Six Steps to Excellence

IN MINISTRY

Kenneth Copeland

KENNETH
COPELAND
PUBLICATIONS

Six Steps to Excellence in Ministry

ISBN-10 1-57562-104-5
ISBN-13 978-1-57562-104-3   30-0025

19 18 17 16 15 14   21 20 19 18 17 16

© 1987 Eagle Mountain International Church Inc. aka Kenneth Copeland Ministries

Kenneth Copeland Publications
Fort Worth, TX 76192-0001

For more information about Kenneth Copeland Ministries, visit kcm.org or call 1-800-600-7395 (U.S. only) or +1-817-852-6000.

Contents

Introduction

Excellence in ministry...
Whatever price it takes, pay it.
The dividends are out of this world!

As Christians, we demand excellence from our heavenly Father. We expect nothing less than total dedication, commitment, reliability and success from a holy, righteous God. We are not looking for failure in God. Divinity and fallibility are incompatible.

We have every right to expect the very best from God. He, Himself, has set the standard of excellence for us. He is our ultimate example of complete success. Since we expect excellence from God, we should also be willing to demand that same excellence from ourselves.

Just as the Lord has called us into Christian ministry and service, He also has called us to reach for perfection in our vocation. "Be ye therefore perfect, even as your Father which is in heaven is perfect" (Matthew 5:48). *"I therefore, the prisoner of the Lord, beseech you that ye walk worthy of the vocation wherewith ye are called"* (Ephesians 4:1). We are also required to demand excellence from those placed in our charge.

If you are a pastor, you are required by God to demand excellence out of your congregation as well as those who work with you in your ministry. As a minister called out on the field, you will demand excellence from the people who work for you and from the congregations you serve. We must be willing to demand the highest form of excellence from the ministries we are involved in.

The Apostle Paul recognized the gravity of his calling. He knew that the gospel was committed into his trust. "...
According to the glorious gospel of the blessed God, which was committed to my trust" (1 Timothy 1:11). Paul took the training of his disciples very seriously because he realized that they were handling the mightiest power in the universe. He wrote, *"For I am not ashamed of the gospel of Christ: for it is the power of God unto salvation to every one that believeth"* (Romans. 1:16). The gospel is the power of God! *The gospel is not only the power by which a person is saved from hell, it is also God's unlimited ability to save, heal and deliver.*

As ministers of the gospel, we are entrusted with God's strength and might. We are therefore faced with two responsibilites:

(1) to develop and maintain excellence of ministry and

(2) to deal with Satan.

Excellence in ministry absolutely will not tolerate unbelief, failure or "taking the easy way out." A ministry of excellence will pay whatever price it takes to get the job done God's way. Our ministries represent Jesus Christ to the world. Ours is a sacred calling. It must be executed with dedication and integrity. We are expected to demonstrate absolute honesty and commitment. *Without a firm decision to succeed with God's help, we cannot hope to maintain the measure of maturity and perfection that our ministry must command.*

Having acknowledged the call and anointing of God upon our life, we pose a serious threat to Satan. In his eyes, we have become the most dangerous living things on this globe. *Our second responsibility is to contend with him.*

Satan is not worried about God. He is postponing that inevitable confrontation as long as he can. But since we represent God's divine power and authority in this world, the adversary *must* reckon with *us*. If a person were to die now, the devil would not care whether he went to heaven or hell. Either way, he would be forever removed from the field of battle and out of his way. What Satan *does* fear is a person who is alive, one who has God's divine nature in his spirit. Only such a person can wield the sword of the spirit—the Word of God—with accuracy. We are dangerous to him, and we will have to resist him.

When we strap on the full armor of God (Ephesians 6:11), we must be prepared and determined to use it. The evil one will certainly attack us with all the forces of darkness. At the same time be prepared for victory! *All of the combined forces of hell are not powerful enough to defeat us!*

The armory of the devil and of his cohorts is restricted to that which is common to man (1 Corinthians 10:13). He cannot go back into his knowledge of spiritual warfare and make use of supernatural weaponry. His power and his arms are limited! Satan has no secret tactics to call upon to prevail against us if we will but stand firm. The God-given weapons of *our* warfare are powerful through God to the pulling down of strongholds (2 Corinthians 10:4). He is limited. We are not.

The victory is ours! First John 4:4 and 1 Corinthians 15:57 guarantee it: *"...Greater is he that is in you, than he that is in the world...thanks be to God, which giveth us the victory through our Lord Jesus Christ."*

In the following pages, I have outlined six basic steps to assure excellence in ministry. Read and study them prayerfully. Learn them. Live by them. Your success will be assured. You have my word on it. But most importantly, you have God's Word on it because His Word is the authority on which they are all based.

Step One:
Dedication—It's Your Decision

The first step to excellence in ministry is dedication. True dedication is a decision of quality—a decision where there is no turning back.

True dedication simply makes a decision based on one's commitment to God, not on feelings or emotions.

The difference between operating on a decision for dedication as opposed to operating by your emotions can be illustrated like this.

Many people pray and beg God to give them a burden for souls, an overwhelming feeling that will *make* them win the lost. Such praying is foolish in light of the teachings of the New Testament. Nowhere are we told to pray this way. We are, however, commanded by Jesus Christ Himself to *"go ye into all the world, and preach the gospel to every creature"* (Mark 16:15). The very fact that a person prays for a burden is evidence that he already has a heart to win souls. All he has to do is obey the commandment. If Jesus told us to do it, that should be sufficient motivation whether we feel like it or not.

The Bible says that Jesus was moved by compassion. What is compassion? It is love. Likewise, God is love. Therefore, compassion is a Person. If Compassion told us to go, then we should be moved by Compassion and pursue the task. We should be moved by what God has said, not by feelings.

Just as a marriage union is solidified by a commitment of faith instead of emotions, the stability of your ministry does not depend on your feelings. A decision for a ministry of excellence is a deep, firm resolution which men cannot alter and circumstances cannot change.

True commitment can be compared to a pilot in a single-engine airplane. If the engine fails in midair, the pilot is committed to landing his craft. He has no choice; his feelings of fear, doubt or inadequacy are of absolutely no consequence whatsoever. He *will* land his plane one way or another. If he has committed himself to flying he will take control and land the best he can and spare his life as well as the lives of his passengers.

A time will come in your life when you will face commitment. *How you handle it now may well determine whether you succeed or fail and even whether you live or die.*

If you are not willing to face commitment, in spite of emergencies and opposition, do not pursue the ministry any longer in that condition. Take the time to get before God and study His Word until the Holy Spirit and you deal with your willingness to be committed. Philippians 2:13 tells you that God is at work in you to both *will* and do His good pleasure. He is faithful, and He will create in you the power and the desire to make an uncompromised decision.

When you finally make a full, no quit, no turning back, forever commitment to God, fulfilling your calling will be the most exciting thing you've ever done. But until the issue is forever settled in your mind and heart, you will have hell on earth. Satan will torment you unmercifully.

Don't be afraid to accept the responsibility of making a decision. God has provided the power, furnished the weapons and equipped you with everything you need. It is the same as experiencing the new birth. *Once you made the decision, God did the rest.* His power, His Spirit and His Word performed their functions, and you were born again. *A decision was all it took.* All you must do is determine in your heart to obey your calling, and God will do His part.

A man once asked me what I did for a living. I answered, "I am a preacher." "Oh," he replied, "yes, I had an uncle who was in the ministry. My, it's a difficult life and a high price to pay." I said, "No, frankly I am having the time of my life."

Never be deceived by thinking that being in the will of God is expensive. The most costly thing on this planet is being *out* of the will of God. *You cannot afford it.*

Find Your Place in the Body

The Bible says that the callings of God are without repentance (Romans 11:29). If you are called to be an apostle, prophet, evangelist, pastor, teacher or to any other ministry in the Body of Christ, the Lord will not revoke the assignment given to you. He ordained you before the foundation of the world. When you stand before the judgment seat of Christ, it will be in the light of your calling—not what you did, nor what you meant to do or wished you had done, but what *God* said you were appointed to do. This applies not only to the fivefold ministry but to every member of Christ's body.

Each believer is anointed and endued with power to fulfill a specific function. By the Spirit of God, every individual is able to perform their calling with mastery and excellence. So, it would be to your advantage to find your calling and get in it!

You may have to change your thinking to find your place. If you have some unscriptural religious traditions, you will have to discard them. For example, 2 Timothy 2:20 says, *"But in a great house there are not only vessels of gold and of silver, but also of wood and of earth; and some to honour, and some to dishonour."* Many who read that verse (or preach it) stop right there. They say, "Not everybody can have the kind of excellent ministry that people like Brother Copeland has because in a great house there are some vessels to honor and some to dishonor. Some are vessels of gold, but some of us are required to be the earthen vessels."

Nonsense! Satan will twist the very scriptures themselves in order to keep people bowed down and trying to please God on the basis of their feelings and false humility. If you don't believe that's hypocritical, just see how you react when someone else starts telling you how worthless you are! Just let your darling child come home from school one day and say, "Guess what the teacher told me today? That I am unworthy, no good and a worm!" You would go to court over that! Yet many people tell God that very thing about themselves and call it humility—that's hypocrisy.

Let's read on and finish the entire passage. Let's see what the Bible actually says about us. *"If a man therefore purge himself from these, he shall be a vessel unto honour, sanctified, and meet for the master's use, and prepared unto every good work"* (verse 21). "Meet" is an Old English word which means "able."

Whether you become a gold pot or a mud pot is *not* the Master's decision; *it is yours*. Both are available. You can be a vessel of honor as a matter of choice.

God has more respect for us than many of us give Him credit for. Did you ever watch a master craftsman at his trade? How does he treat his tools? He is not negligent and careless. His tools are specially designed and tempered, full of strength and power to do very specific tasks. As a skilled craftsman, he depends upon his instruments for his livelihood. He meticulously uses, cares for and maintains the tools of his trade. They are extensions of his creativity. He intends for them to last a lifetime and to be handed down to his son after him. The tools of a man's trade take care of him, and he takes care of them.

In the redemption of the human race, you and I are the tools of God's craft. Jesus is the Redeemer, but we are the bearers of good news. He is the vine, but we are the branches that bear the fruit. He will care for us and sustain us. He will temper us. A wrench is not tempered by beating it over an anvil. People have the mistaken idea that to strengthen a believer

God has to beat and harass him.

No! It takes oil to temper steel. The oil of the Holy Spirit toughens and reinforces us. Our strength and power lie in the Word of God and His Spirit indwelling us.

Devote Yourself to Pleasing God

A decision for total dedication includes a determination to please God. Go through the New Testament and learn those things that bring Him pleasure. For instance, *"But without faith it is impossible to please him"* (Hebrews 11:6). We must walk by faith in order to please God.

The Father God is not delighted when we are in the flesh. We must be spiritually minded (Romans 8:1-8).

God receives no enjoyment out of our being defeated. Defeated Christians do not delight their heavenly Father. He was grieved at the children of Israel because they were overcome in the wilderness. *"For some, when they had heard, did provoke: howbeit not all that came out of Egypt by Moses. But with whom was he grieved forty years? was it not with them that had sinned, whose carcases fell in the wilderness?"* (Hebrews 3:16-17). *Our not walking in victory is just as offensive to Him.*

The decision to please the Father must include the decision to live in victory. The victory which overcomes the world is faith (1 John 5:4). God intends for you to use your faith for every endeavor in life. You should bat your eyes by faith! *"The just shall live by faith"* (Romans 1:17).

In addition to faith, you must also live and walk in the love of God. Getting strife out of your life is part of your dedication to God. That, my friend, requires a firm, quality decision of the highest order.

In my own ministry at times, I know I must appear two-faced to those who work around me. I demand excellence. Yet on the other hand, I will be supportive of a person who is falling far short of perfection in his work. Because of my commitment to walk in the love of God, I'll stay with him and stand by him. I have had people ask me why I did not dismiss someone from my staff because of their incompetence. I am simply not that type. As long as a person is making every effort to succeed, I will work with him to see that he attains the accuracy and perfection he is capable of with God's help.

But there is one thing which we do not allow in our ministry. If a person causes strife, he'll have to work someplace else. We absolutely will not tolerate strife because it is so destructive.

Notice again 2 Timothy 2:21, *"If a man therefore purge himself from these...."* What are the "these" to which Paul refers? Verses 22-24 tells us, *"Flee also youthful lusts: but follow righteousness, faith, charity [love], peace, with them that call on the Lord out of a pure heart. But foolish and unlearned questions avoid, knowing that they do gender strifes. And the servant of the Lord must not strive."*

Avoiding strife is not a suggestion; it is a command. The servant of the Lord must not be in strife. You are a servant of the Lord, so you cannot quarrel, bicker and fight with *anyone.* *"But be gentle unto all men, apt to teach, patient, in meekness instructing those that oppose themselves* [or those that are in strife and opposition to one another]; *if God peradventure will give them repentance to the acknowledging of the truth; and that they may recover themselves out of the snare of the devil, who are taken captive by him at his will"* (2 Timothy 2:24-26).

You cannot afford strife. It will cause you to be taken captive by Satan at Satan's will. You are no longer a civilian. You are a soldier of the Cross. You have answered the call and taken your place in the ranks of the forces of Almighty God. Put on the armor and fight the good fight of faith. *If you surrender to the enemy, you will be worthless to the kingdom of God.* The last thing God needs is for His army to become prisoners of war!

When you are not walking in love and have strife in your life, the gifts of the Spirit are stopped. First Corinthians 13:1-3 says,

Though I speak with tongues of men and of angels, and have not charity [love], I am become as sounding brass, or a tinkling cymbal. And though I have the gift of prophecy, and understand all mysteries, and all knowledge; and though I have all faith, so that I could remove mountains, and have not charity [love], I am nothing. And though I bestow all my goods to feed the poor, and though I give my body to be burned, and have not charity [love], it profiteth me nothing.

The words of wisdom and of knowledge, the gift of faith, gifts of healing, working of miracles, discerning of spirits, tongues and interpretation of tongues and prophecy are nine weapons of our warfare. If Satan attacks them individually, he has nine fights on his hands. *All he has to do to defeat all of them in one stroke is simply cause strife among those who are operating in the gifts.* Think about that in the light of James 3:16: *"Where there is strife, there is confusion and every evil work."* No wonder there has been so much confusion connected with the operation of the gifts of the Spirit.

Stand on the Word of God and take control of your feelings. *Strife is born in the emotions.* To control your emotions, *you must control your tongue.* The Bible says that the person who can control his words can gain mastery over his entire body (James 3:2).

Be dedicated.

Decide to please the Father.

Decide to live in victory.

Decide to walk the life of love.

Decide to live by faith.

Make the quality, no-turning-back decision that if your faith won't get it, then you won't have it—because you are determined to live by faith!

Satan will see to it that sooner or later you will come to a place where you will have to make the choice. Don't ever make the choice to do it the easy way and not believe God for it. When it comes down to it, stand on the Word and use your faith. *Always take the Word way.* Always take the faith way. Stand immovable on the promises of God.

Commit Yourself to a Life of Prayer

Prayer is the foundation for success in every Christian endeavor. Jesus is your example. Did you ever notice how often the Bible mentions that He withdrew to a lonely place to pray? *"And in the morning, rising up a great while before day, he went out, and departed into a solitary place, and there prayed"* (Mark 1:35). *"And it came to pass in those days, that he went out into a mountain to pray, and continued all night in prayer to God"* (Luke 6:12). These are just two of many instances recorded in the Gospels.

Jesus was in *continual communication* with God through prayer. He spent hours every day separated from the people, fellowshiping with His heavenly Father. *If He had a need for preparation through prayer, how much more should we?* In fact, such foundation and preparation is the only thing that will keep us together when we are faced with a situation that requires a great deal of faith. Even the apostles chose deacons to assist them in their duties, saying, *"It is not reason that we should leave the word of God.... But we will give ourselves continually to prayer, and to the ministry of the word"* (Acts 6:2, 4).

If you have taken the time to saturate your heart with the Word of God to the extent that you are *single-minded* on His

Word, your thinking will no longer be influenced by fear. You will stop wailing and begging God for the power to do the job. You will realize that *"the anointing which ye have received of him abideth in you"* (1 John 2:27). All you will have to do is open your mouth, *"For out of the abundance of the heart the mouth speaketh"* (Matthew 12:34). The Word will be what's in your heart in abundance, so that's what will come out.

When some mother brings her little baby to you whom Satan has maimed, twisted and blinded, you will know what to do. You won't offer a lame excuse like, "Well, you know, sometimes we just don't understand why these things happen. Sometimes we just have no answer." If that is your response, then go hide behind a desk someplace! Shuffle papers and organize bake sales and softball matches against the church down the street!

God will heal that baby if you have the courage to stand up to the devil. That kind of confidence only comes from a personal knowledge of God through time spent in prayer and fellowship with Him.

Once a woman brought a little whisper of a baby to me in a meeting. Its tiny feet were so badly twisted that that the toes on each foot touched the backs of its legs. The mother was looking to me to do something about it. In a situation like that you need to be in close contact with the Father.

When she handed me her little baby, I started to pray. It was so tiny that both feet fit in the palm of my hand. I said,

"Father, in the Name of Jesus...." That's as far as I got, and I felt those little feet turn around in my hand.

I would rather be anointed of God for five minutes than to have a gold fence built around the entire state of Texas with my name on every brick. It is the greatest thing on earth. *The hours of prayer and communion with God are worth the results they bring.*

The demonstration of God's power in your ministry is proof of your personal fellowship with Him. You cannot have one without the other.

Step Two:
Singleness of Purpose

Our single purpose as ministers of God is to meet the needs of the people. James 1:5-8 tells us why single-mindedness is so important.

If any of you lack wisdom, let him ask of God, that giveth to all men liberally, and upbraideth not; and it shall be given him. But let him ask in faith, nothing wavering. For he that wavereth is like a wave of the sea driven with the wind and tossed. For let not that man think that he shall receive any thing of the Lord.

"A double minded man is unstable in all his ways" (verse 8). The Amplified Bible says, "[For being as he is] a man of two minds (hesitating...)." What happens when you hesitate? Your adversary takes the first step. You find yourself on the defensive with Satan ahead of you beating you at every turn. If you are not single-minded about your purpose for being in the ministry, you will not have any definite direction. You will always be wondering what you are supposed to do.

Don't Hesitate to Step Out on Your Faith

Do you remember when you felt the first symptom of a

cold or the flu strike you and you waited around for two or three days before you picked up your Bible and prayed about it? Then, later on you wondered why you waited until you were sick before you acted. Your hesitation gave the sickness an opportunity to get a hold on you. Hesitating is *not* a quality of a single-minded person. It is *"...a man of two minds—hesitating, dubious, irresolute..."* (James 1:8, *The Amplified Bible*).

Irresolute means indecisive, a man who has not thoroughly resolved things in his mind and settled them once and for all. *"... [He is] unstable and unreliable and uncertain about everything [he thinks, feels, decides]"* (James 1:8, *The Amplified Bible*).

If a man is of two minds, then the decisions he makes are split. When you get into an area of indecision, you are at a standstill. You won't go either way.

A double-minded man is one who tries to live by faith and protects his fear at the same time. He talks both ways. His faith proclaims, "I believe God is going to heal you someday." Then his fear whispers, "But I wouldn't want to say that you are well just yet." *Inconsistency is hazardous.* If you are hesitating in stepping out on your faith in ministry, your adversary will always be one step ahead of you. You will never see the power of God work through you to heal anyone.

The eighth chapter of Luke records an event in the life of Christ which illustrates the danger of instability and hesitancy.

Now it came to pass on a certain day, that he went into a ship with his disciples: and he said unto them, Let us go over unto the other side of the lake. And they launched forth. But as they sailed he fell asleep: and there came down a storm of wind on the lake; and they were filled with water, and were in jeopardy. And they came to him, and awoke him, saying, Master, master, we perish. Then he arose, and rebuked the wind and the raging of the water: and they ceased, and there was a calm. And he said unto them, Where is your faith? And they being afraid wondered, saying one to another, What manner of man is this! for he commandeth even the winds and water, and they obey him (Luke 8:22-25).

Jesus stated when they first entered the ship, *"Let us go over unto the other side of the lake"* (verse 22). There was enough power in those words to have gotten the disciples all the way across the lake. Yet, they became afraid and ran to waken Jesus crying, *"Master, master, we perish"* (verse 24). Here is a perfect illustration of double-mindedness. They were speaking death to the Author of life. They were speaking fear in the very presence of faith personified, the Son of the living God. They were consumed with the problem while the Solution Himself slept in their vessel.

We perish didn't sound unstable to them, but to Jesus, it was a direct contradiction of what He had stated. When Jesus said to them, *"Let us go over unto the other side of the lake"* (Luke 8:22). He knew without a shadow of a doubt where they were going. The disciples should have known too. They should have stood in the bow of that ship and shouted out, "The Son of the living God, the Christ, has told us to go over to the other side. Now, peace, be still!" If they were not capable of exercising such faith, Jesus would not have had the right to rebuke them after He stilled the storm. *"Why are ye so fearful? How is it that ye have no faith?"* (Mark 4:40).

The disciples were filled with wonder and astonishment. *"What manner of man is this, that even the wind and the sea obey him"* (verse 41)? Jesus had just spent an entire day expounding on the power of God to these men and instructing them in what the Word would do. Then, when He demonstrated it before their eyes, they were dumbfounded. Instead of standing on the Word as He did, they were double-minded.

A single-minded man is a man that makes quality decisions and settles them forever. If you are going to put the Lord, His work and Word first in your life, there will be times when you will have to bypass what you see in order to meet the people's needs. *Don't hesitate. Do whatever it takes.*

Preach the Word in Season and Out

As the Apostle Paul instructed young Timothy, *"Preach the word; be instant in season, out of season...do the work of an evangelist, make full proof of thy ministry"* (2 Timothy 4:2, 5).

Preach the Word. When your congregation says, "We've got financial problems," don't hesitate. Deliver the gospel. When you have a building program to complete, preach the Word. When your church says, "It can't be done," get with it. Don't spend your time trying to figure out how to get things done or how to get people to give. *If no one is giving, then you are not preaching the Word.* People will support you if you feed them spiritually.

You may say, "But I have no place to preach!" Preach it on the street corner if you must, but do it! Minister to everyone you meet, everywhere you go!

I have known many very good, well-intentioned men who have sought God's anointing by praying earnestly, *Oh, God, I've got to have Your power manifest in my ministry!* They have spent hours and days praying, interceding and fasting. Every minister wants God's power and the gifts of the Spirit to manifest through them. Some would give anything in this world if someone they laid hands on would fall out under the power of God! You can beg until you change color, *but it's only when you start preaching the Word that the power begins.* Your job is to meet the needs of the people. *The Word of God has the answer to every need. When you deliver the Word, signs will follow.*

When you roll all the care of it over on God and simply say, "Well, Lord, You want them saved more than I do. You want them healed worse than I do. You want their needs met more than I, so I'm just going to preach the Word. I'll preach it in season and out of season. I'll preach it at night. The only thing I'll ever be accused of doing too much is preaching the Word! Whether they respond or not, I'll preach the Word! I will not be swayed by anything or anybody; I will preach the Word!"

Preach it to yourself first and then to everybody you come in contact with. Be willing to walk away from ANYTHING in order to get God's Word to others. When you make that kind of decision, I promise you by the authority of the written Holy Word of God that signs will follow your ministry, the necessary funds will come in, and you will have more places to preach than you can handle.

If you have one dollar, use it to share the gospel. If you have a thousand dollars, use it to minister the Word. If you have a hundred thousand dollars, use it to fulfill your calling.

When you get through, preach some more. When you get tired, when you don't feel well, and even when you feel better, *GO PREACH!*

God's Word is all you need. The Scriptures will save you, heal you, fill you with the Holy Spirit. They will turn you into the righteousness of God and meet your needs according to His riches in glory. The Word of God will sustain you in every way. *"So then faith cometh by hearing, and hearing by the word of God"* (Romans 10:17). A man filled with faith can do ANYTHING *HE CAN BELIEVE.* All things are possible to him who believes.

If there is ever a choice between the Word and *anything* else, choose the Bible way. If you are a musician and God uses you in music, put the gospel to music. Whatever talent God has given you, use it to preach the good news!

God sticks by the Book. You stay with the Word, and God will stay with you. The Bible says that He is *"upholding all things by the word of his power"* (Hebrews 1:3). If you want to be upheld, then get on His promises!

Step Three:
Follow the Leadership
of the Holy Spirit

In ministering, never follow the path your mind wants to take. *Don't lean to your own understanding. Learn to follow the leadership of the Holy Spirit within you.* He is there inside you to lead you.

I remember when I first started in the ministry. I had been preaching for about two years in various churches, usually ones in which no one else would preach.

Then one day the Lord spoke to me to get out of those churches and to start holding some meetings of my own. I prayed about it, and the Lord led me to Wichita Falls, Texas. I rented an old, abandoned drugstore building and some folding chairs.

On one Wednesday night, I remember that the anointing was really strong. I preached on the reality of the righteousness of God. It was going great, and I was having the time of my life. But just as I built my sermon up to its climactic moment and God was just coming forth with the finish, a woman in the audience suddenly burst forth in tongues.

I felt like someone had stood up and doused me with a fire hose. I said, "Lady, hold that." She just kept on. Again, "Lady, hold that until I finish." She got a little louder. I shouted, "In the Name of Jesus, shut up!" She grew louder still. By this time the service was in shambles. I finally just stood back and let her go on and on and on. It seemed to me that she went on for an hour and a half. Then she shifted over in English, "Yea, yea, saith the Lord...." She never said anything intelligible.

This continued on for what seemed like an eternity. After a while, everyone was squirming around in their seats. They looked like they were about ready to wring her neck. Finally, when she hushed, I looked right at her and I said sternly, "Well, we've already lost what we were studying anyway, so I am going to teach you something. You wouldn't have had the nerve to interrupt me in English while I was preaching, so why would you do it in a language you don't understand?"

About that time, a man sitting next to her spoke up and said, "Brother Copeland, she is stone deaf. She didn't hear a word you said."

What do you do faced with a situation like that? Whatever you say can and will be held against you. What is there to say anyway?

I found out later that someone had planned the whole thing. They had already run half a dozen preachers out of town with the same trick. She was being used by some very selfish people. It was set up that when the man next to her punched her with his elbow, it was "her turn" to prophesy.

During times likes these, your decision to meet the needs of the people *must* rise to the surface. Jesus said that the Holy

Spirit would lead us into all truth and that His sheep would know His voice. I was determined that no demonic spirit would run me out of town.

It was so heavy in there, so quiet. Everybody was just waiting to see what I would do. I just closed my eyes and inside my own consciousness I said, "Lord, you will have to show me what to do. I am not going to make a move until you tell me what I am to do."

The answer came to me. It was so simple that my carnal mind would never have thought of it. I would not have even acted on it if *I* had thought of it!

The Lord said, "Call her up and lay hands on her, and I will open her ears." I said to the man next to her, "Sir, bring her up here. I am going to lay my hands on her, and God will open her ears." He would not budge, so I called her up myself and laid hands on her, and God opened her ears.

I finished my sermon on righteousness, and we had a marvelous time under the anointing of God. The meeting grew, and that old drugstore soon filled up. We had a glorious time, and many received from God.

If you are going to minister to people's needs, you will have to be led of the Holy Spirit because more often than not you will find yourself in situations that only His wisdom can handle.

Some years later, I was preaching in Fort Worth, Texas. There were about 2,000 people in attendance one evening.

Among them, unknown to me, was a witch who had brought a human chalice with her. A human chalice is a person used by witches to receive and accumulate demonic spirits. (You may encounter some of these people some day.) They attend gospel meetings for the very purpose of gathering demonic spirits that are cast out of others.

I realize that to many people, the idea of witches and witchcraft may seem ridiculous. Unfortunately, however, these things *do* exist. *We, as ministers of Jesus Christ, will have to contend with them, just as our Lord dealt with them.*

This witch sat across the aisle from the chalice and was using her to create a disturbance in that meeting. Every child in the place was crying. Everyone was restless and moving about. Unless a situation like that is controlled quickly, a whole service will be ruined.

When these types of instances arise, you must also be prepared beforehand. Unless you have spent time in prayer, you will not be able to effectively deal with those situations.

You can forget about being led of the Holy Spirit if you spend your preparation time tending to personal affairs, playing golf with influential people, making business appointments, and selling your tapes and records. Hire someone else who is anointed to handle those things. *Spend your time in prayer and in the Word before a meeting.* Otherwise, you will simply not be spiritually prepared to minister the Word and to overcome the obstacles which Satan will surely throw in your path. Don't ever substitute hard work for prayer.

When this disturbance arose that evening, I asked the Lord, "What should I do?" He said, *Bind that disturbance.* Many times it will not even be necessary for you to speak aloud, just under your breath, "In the Name of Jesus."

In this particular case (and this is why you must listen to the Spirit of God), I was to bind the disturbance. So I said, "You spirit of disturbance, in the Name of Jesus Christ of Nazareth, I take complete and total authority over you now, and I cast you out of this place!"

Every child in that auditorium hushed. The whole audience became quiet and still. One of our ushers had spotted the chalice and had come and stood behind her without her being aware of his presence. He heard her whispering to the evil spirit, "Come on back! Come on back!" Finally, she became so upset she screamed, got up and ran out of the building. When that happened, the witch jumped up and ran out behind her. They fled so fast that they ran into my son in the lobby and knocked him down.

Right at that moment my mind went totally and completely blank. I could not remember what I had been preaching. What do you do in a case like that?

Thank God, I don't have to speak out of my mind. I just started preaching in tongues at the direction of the Holy Spirit. All the time the scripture kept running through me that says, *"Wherefore let him that speaketh in an unknown tongue pray that he may interpret*" (1 Corinthians 14:13).

I had not spoken very long in tongues before I changed over into English. I preached in English for about 40 minutes and had no idea what I was saying. At the end of that time, it was just as though I had come right back to the place I had left off. Suddenly, I remembered the very last word I had spoken 40 minutes before. I took the next word, finished the sentence, kept right on preaching and completed that sermon.

We had one of the most anointed services that evening that we had ever had. Later on by listening to the cassette tape of that service, I discovered what I had said during the 40 minute interval when I had spoken solely by the Anointing of the Spirit.

In order for you, as a minister, to be able to be led of God, you will have to be attuned to the Holy Spirit. You cannot lean to your own understanding. You must be totally grounded in and dependent upon the Word of God. You must *"let the word of Christ dwell in you richly in all wisdom"* (Colossians 3:16).

Don't Be Influenced by Situations

On another occasion I was preaching in Jamaica. Sometimes, it is so dark at night there that you can't see the outline of your hand in front of your face. I was up in the mountains. About 150 people were gathered in one small room, so jam-packed that they could hardly move. Everyone except me was black, and the room itself was in total darkness except for a kerosene lantern. It was hung over my head so that I could read my Bible. All I could see was my Bible and the feet of the man right in front of me—not his face, just his feet.

The first ten to fifteen minutes was the most difficult preaching I have ever done in my life. I began to realize how much I depended upon the facial expressions of the audience. *As I was preaching, I noticed that people's reactions determined how my sermon was being received. I could adjust my message or delivery accordingly.* I never realized that I had been doing that.

I stopped quietly for a moment and in my own spirit I said, "In the Name of Jesus, I make this firm quality decision: For the rest of my ministry, *I will never preach another sermon except by faith. I will not be swayed by the expressions of people."* I finished ministering that night and had a glorious time doing it.

Later on I learned that even if I had been able to see their expressions, I might have misinterpreted their reaction to the gospel message. The Jamaicans have been so influenced by British tradition and custom that they show very little expression at all.

If something *did* happen to one of them during a service, it was their custom to go to the pastor after the meeting and inform him privately of what had occurred. He could then pass the information on to the visiting minister, if he so chose.

One lady had been completely healed of blindness during one of our meetings. She never let on that anything had taken place. It took her some time to work up the nerve to come and tell me about it. She was almost rigid. She found me outside and said simply, "Brother Copeland, I was blind but now I can see. Thank you." That was all. A miracle had taken place, and yet she *seemed* totally unemotional about it. So I learned another valuable lesson from this experience. *Don't be influenced by emotional reactions or physical expressions of the people while you are ministering the Word. Be totally led and motivated by the Holy Spirit.*

Be Prepared for Disturbances

From Jamaica I came back to Little Rock, Arkansas, the following week. I was preaching in a place provided for us by the Dairyman's Association. Suddenly one evening, every light in the place went out. The sound system, the air conditioning, the tape recorder and everything else went completely off. It was totally dark.

Your first reaction in the natural is to stop and say something like, "What happened to the lights?" Don't stop preaching regardless of what happens or what anybody else does. *Never let disturbances stop you unless it is a situation in which you have to deal with people.* Then just pause long enough to find out what the Spirit of God says to do about it, but don't be caught at a loss for what to say or do. *In every disturbance, the confession of your heart and mouth ought to be, "I am led by the Spirit of God. I am a son of God, and I am more than a conqueror in this situation."*

As I continued, I could hear the people snickering. They

didn't know what to do. Finally, God's Spirit said to me, *Give an invitation to receive the Holy Ghost.* I did. Three people came up, and I laid hands on them. I could barely see their outlines, but they all received the Holy Spirit.

When the lights came back, I acted as though nothing had happened. Everybody else may want to acknowledge the situation. If you don't do it, they will follow your lead. *You are in charge of that service, so **you** be the master of it. Keep control at all times.*

You should know everything that is happening in that meeting. That is the reason why you should spend the hours that it takes to be quiet and open your spirit to God and listen to Him. Then you will be spiritually prepared for whatever arises. You will be able to follow the lead of the Holy Spirit.

God's principal method of guiding His people, individually and collectively, is through the ministry of His Holy Spirit—not by prophecies, dreams, visions or other "supernatural" phenomena. He may choose to speak or lead through one or more of these channels and on occasion does so. But that is not His best. Jesus said, *"Howbeit when he, the Spirit of truth, is come, he will guide you…"*(John 16:13). This is God's way of leadership in our lives. To enjoy excellence in your calling, you must depend on the guidance of the Holy Spirit.

Step Four:
Strip Away the Things of the World

Just before His crucifixion, Jesus prayed a special prayer for His disciples. He said, *"They are not of the world, even as I am not of the world. Sanctify them through thy truth: thy word is truth"* (John 17:16, 17).

To *sanctify* means "to separate unto." We are *in* this world but not *of* it. *So to have excellence of ministry, we must strip away everything of the world from our lives until there is nothing left but the Word of God.*

One of the first things that must be rooted out is our sin. We must cease confessing our sin consciousness and stop preaching that we are "just old sinners saved by grace." We *were* old sinners; but since we have been saved, we are now made the righteousness of God. *"For he [God] hath made him [Jesus] to be sin for us, who knew no sin; that we might be made the righteousness of God in him"* (2 Corinthians 5:21).

Stop seeing yourself or other Christians as "reformed" sinners—all are now the very righteousness of God. Look at yourself and other believers that way. Emphasize your right-standing with God. *When you minister to your congregation, teach them who they are in Christ and what a glorious inheritance they have right now because of what He has done for us.*

Second, strip away your negative confessions. Don't confess that you are sinful, needy, weak or sick. Find out what God has said about you and confess the truth. *You are what the Word says you are.*

You are redeemed from the curse of the law. Make Galatians 3:13-14 your constant confession to yourself and to your congregation. *"Christ hath redeemed us from the curse of the law, being made a curse for us.... That the blessing of Abraham might come on the Gentiles through Jesus Christ."*

What is the blessing of Abraham? *Health, prosperity, success, wisdom, righteousness.* (See Deuteronomy 28:1-14.) *Confess these things!*

Jesus said:

For out of the abundance of the heart the mouth speaketh. A good man out of the good treasure of the heart bringeth forth good things: and an evil man out of the evil treasure bringeth forth evil things. But I say unto you, That every idle word that men shall speak, they shall give account thereof in the day of judgment. For by thy words thou shalt be justified, and by thy words thou shalt be condemned (Matthew 12:34-37).

Learn to control your speech. Watch out for verbal expressions and clichés like "I was scared to death." "That tickled me to death." "I could have died." Do it out of respect for Jesus. *You of all people ought to know that you can have what you say.* Besides, it is simply not true. You were not scared or tickled to the point of dying; you were not at all on the verge of death.

When you have grown to the point in your spiritual life where you have confidence in the integrity of your own word, you won't have any difficulty believing that God's Word is good. Then, you will eliminate those "idle words."

As a minister of the gospel, you set the example; you must make absolutely certain that what you say is true and honest. If you want God to bless what you preach, you will have to put away exaggeration and telling stories that are just not so.

I am speaking from experience. We have all heard this type of "evangelistic talk" at one time or another. That is the same kind of "trade puffery" used by Madison Avenue in every radio and television commercial we hear. *Never be guilty of sounding like used-car salesmen and carnival barkers.*

When we say that we had "better'n eight hundred" in a meeting, many times that means there were only 450 in attendance. When a handful are saved, we say that we had a "landslide" of souls brought into the kingdom. A man of the Word dares not engage in such self-delusion. *"For by thy words thou shalt be justified, and by thy words thou shalt be condemned"* (Matthew 12:37).

Do Away With Spiritual Junk Food

Put the Word of God first place in your life and allow it to strip away all the other things. *It won't work while you sit and watch television day and night.* Break the habit.

I, at one time, loved to read the newspaper. Through the years, it almost became an addiction. I *had* to read it every day. There is nothing wrong with watching television or reading the paper, but it is not necessary that we do so. It may be detrimental to our spiritual lives. Jesus said the cares of the world will choke the Word (Mark 4:19).

Paul wrote to young Timothy, "...*be a good minister of Jesus Christ, nourished up in the words of faith and of good doctrine*" (1 Timothy 4:6). We should be spiritually nourished every day. A steady diet of the mass media is harmful to our spiritual health and growth just as a "junk food" diet is to our physical bodies. We cannot "feed" off of TV and be "good ministers of Jesus Christ."

The media generally dwells on the negative side of life—wars, inflation, accidents, death, conflicts—and the Bible tells us that the cares of this world will choke the Word (Matthew 13:22).

In 1967, I made a decision to fast my newspaper for two weeks and to spend that time in the Word. I have not gone back to the paper yet. Occasionally, I pick up one and look through it, but the attraction is gone. The reason I lost interest is simple: I was getting more out of the Word of God than I was out of the newspaper. It caused the separation I needed.

I am not preaching against reading newspapers. *Ours is not a gospel of "don'ts."* I am emphasizing the fact that I receive more from the Word of God than from any of these other things in life.

I used to derive my satisfaction from things like month-long fishing trips, riding motorcycles, hunting or flying. They are all enjoyable. But now, instead of getting contentment from these things, I am satisfied before I do them. When your Word level gets low and your confession level gets low, then you have a tendency to start seeking something in the natural to satisfy that craving. *It takes the Word of God to separate you from the things of this world.* Unnecessary things take up your time and dilute the power of God operating in and through you.

Put Away Man-made Schemes

As a minister, you cannot be satisfied with being "as honest as the next fellow." You are called to be holy even as God is holy, regardless of what pressures Satan may bring to bear. You have to do "double duty" as a man of God. You must practice what you preach. *Your faith and confidence must rest on the infallible Word of God and not on your own shrewd dealings.*

Let me give you an illustration from my own experience. During a series of meetings we held in Ruston, Louisiana, we were plagued by problems from the beginning. When I arrived, I learned that the building we rented in advance was a "rat trap." It literally smelled like rotten tennis shoes. The crowds were sparse. I was homesick. And the devil was attacking my mind telling me that no one cared about me or my ministry anyway. I discovered during the last meeting that we were still $900 short of meeting our budget. I immediately started wondering how I was going to get the people to give.

I began to act out of fear and panic instead of by faith in the Word of God. I lost sight of the fact that God could send someone to that meeting for the specific purpose of meeting my needs. *By allowing myself to become consumed with the problem, doubt and confusion took over.* If I hadn't straightened up, I would have closed the door to what God wanted to do and would have given Satan the opportunity to intercept that person whom God was sending with the funds. *Doubt could have cost me my victory.*

In desperation I rationalized, *God, now I've been faithful to Your cause. My credit is good. I know what I'll do. I can just get out of town quietly and leave the bills unpaid for just a little while. I can pay them from what I receive from the next meeting.* If I had, I would have wrecked my next budget before I ever got there! That kind of reasoning leads to disaster. Once you start, your downfall is assured—it's just a matter of time.

God is everywhere. He works from both ends of a problem at the same time. Our knowledge and understanding of the situation doesn't even scratch the surface. In cases like this, the Father is trying to get us out of the way, so He can intervene. *His reputation is on the line, not ours. If we will exercise faith and trust, the solution will come.*

I was panicky. *Maybe,* I thought, *if I ran down to the newspaper office and took out a full-page ad, it would attract enough people here tonight to reach that budget.* Satan distracted me from meeting the needs of the people by getting me to think about how I could gather a big enough crowd to bring in the money.

If I had taken out an ad, all I would have done was add another $500 or more to the already fractured budget. I learned that my commitment to "excellence" kept me from leaning on my own understanding.

Lay Aside the Cares of This World

At that same meeting, I also came to understand that I had to let the Word separate me from the cares of this world. With that unmet budget staring me in the face, I got my Bible and turned to every scripture in the Word of God that guaranteed me, by the blood of Jesus, that my expenses were met. Verses like, *"But seek ye first the kingdom of God, and his righteousness; and all these things* [you need] *shall be added unto you"* (Matthew 6:33). *"Ask, and it shall be given you"* (Matthew 7:7). *"But my God shall supply all your need according to his riches in glory by Christ Jesus"* (Philippians 4:19). *"Give, and it shall be given unto you"* (Luke 6:38).

Then I went to 1 Peter 5:7, *"Casting all your care upon him; for he careth for you."* I rolled the care of the expenses over on Him. I promised God that with the Holy Spirit as my Helper I would not touch that problem in my thought life again.

I prepared myself to preach. I told Satan, "If you bother me anymore about this thing, I'll not even take up an offering tonight. I will get it by faith, and when I do, I'll just have added testimony to give in my next meeting."

I wanted to worry so badly! I went into the courtyard of that motel and walked around the swimming pool. Every time I though about the problem, I would say out loud, "No, I have rolled the care of that over on the Lord. I will not think about it. The budget is met." I kept quoting the Word of God to myself and to Satan. I had to keep talking out loud to keep my mind from worrying! *I couldn't worry as long as I had to think about what I was saying.*

After a while, a man drove up in the driveway and began to honk his horn. I saw him but didn't respond because I don't visit with people when I am in prayer or meditation. I tried to ignore him, but he kept honking the horn. Finally, he stuck his head out the window and shouted, *"COME HERE!"* It was with such authority that I obeyed.

He said to me, "Brother Copeland, I'm sorry to disturb you, but I had to get your attention. I'm committed to another obligation and will be late for the meeting tonight. I was afraid I would miss the offering." He handed me a check. I prayed over the gift and shook the man's hand. I went back to my room and opened that check. It was for $500. *The offering in the service that night was for the exact amount I needed for the budget expenses.*

I paid all my bills and left town knowing full well that the

Word works. *There is only one way you will get to the place where people will chase you down to put money into your offering—put the Word of God first place and make it final authority. Strip away everything else but the Word!*

If I had not rid myself of that care and cast it over on God, that need would probably have never been met.

Step Five:
Look to the Word Day and Night

Looking to the Word will produce several effects on your ministry that you cannot get any other way. You will obtain God's favor and you will increase your faith as well as your understanding of how to use your faith. Luke 11:49 refers to the Word of God as His wisdom. Proverbs 4:5-9 reads:

> Get wisdom, get understanding: forget it not; neither decline from the words of my mouth. Forsake her not, and she shall preserve thee: love her, and she shall keep thee. Wisdom is the principal thing; therefore get wisdom: and with all thy getting get understanding. Exalt her, and she shall promote thee: she shall bring thee to honour, when thou dost embrace her. She shall give to thine head an ornament of grace: a crown of glory shall she deliver to thee.

The ornament of grace Solomon referred to is being clothed with the favor of God. It is the result of seeking God's wisdom by exalting His Word which brings divine favor. The wisdom of God places a crown of glory (God's grace or favor) upon a person's head.

That grace, or favor, is available to every person on earth *without exception,* for *"God is no respecter of persons"* (Acts 10:34).

Favor cannot be earned. It is the gift of God. You do not merit it. You receive it. Although it is free, God's grace is *not* automatic. It must be appropriated by the believer *through faith.*

We already know that *"faith cometh by hearing, and hearing by the word of God"* (Romans 10:17). The basis for receiving God's favor is through faith. Therefore, you obtain God's favor through His Word.

God created the heavens and the earth through a combination of His faith, wisdom and understanding (Proverbs 3:19; Hebrews 11:3). In Mark 11:22, Jesus exhorts His disciples, *"Have faith in God."* The marginal note in the *King James Version* reads, *"Have the faith of God."* Another version puts it this way, *"Have the God-kind of faith." The faith that is in us is exactly the same faith that is in God. He gave each of us the same measure of faith* (Romans 12:3).

If God could create the entire universe with His faith, then why are we so limited in our ability to bring things to pass using that same force? Why is God so much more successful than we? Because, He has the wisdom and understanding to use it to its fullest capacity.

Wisdom is the ability to use knowledge. First Corinthians 1:30 tells us that Christ Jesus *"is made unto us wisdom...." He* is our wisdom. *"We have the mind of Christ"* (1 Corinthians 2:16).

Whenever you think of God's wisdom or knowledge, you are thinking of the Word of God. God said:

For my thoughts are not your thoughts, neither are your
ways my ways, saith the Lord. For as the heavens are
higher than the earth, so are my ways higher than your
ways, and my thoughts than your thoughts....so shall my
word be that goeth forth out of my mouth: it shall not
return unto me void, but it shall accomplish that which I
please, and it shall prosper in the thing whereto I sent it
(Isaiah 55:8-9, 11).

In other words God is saying, "Even though I think higher
than you think and My ways are higher than your ways, I give
you My Word so that you will be able to think like I do *and
conform to My ways.*"

The wisdom of God is His written Word. His knowledge is
shared with us through the Word as evidenced by 2 Corinthians
10:5, *"Casting down imaginations, and every high thing that exalt-
eth itself against the knowledge of God, and bringing into captivity
every thought to the obedience of Christ"* (John 1:14). Jesus Christ
is the Word. If Jesus Himself is the Word and if He is made
unto us wisdom, then we can conclude that true wisdom is
the Word of God. *God and His Word agree at all times.*

With these thoughts in mind, let's rephrase Proverbs 4:5-9
in this way:

Get [the Word]: get understanding: forget it not; neither
decline from the words of my mouth. Forsake [the Word

of God] not, and [it] shall...keep thee. [The Word] is the principal thing; therefore get [the Word]: and with all thy getting get understanding. Exalt [the Word], and [it] shall promote thee: [it] shall bring thee to honour, when thou dost embrace [it]. [It] shall give to thine head an ornament of grace: a crown of glory shall [the Word] deliver to thee.

Remember: Look to the Word day and night. Proverbs 4:20-22 says:

My son, attend to my words; incline thine ear unto my sayings. Let them not depart from thine eyes; keep them in the midst of thine heart. For they are life unto those that find them, and health to all their flesh.

Exalt the Word. Let it do the work. If there is ever a problem, apply God's wisdom to it. *Speak and act only on the Word.* If you exalt the Word, people will be delivered.

The Word Promotes

If you will refrain from exalting yourself but instead lift up the Word of God, then it will promote you and bring you to a place of honor. Peter tells us, *"Humble yourselves therefore under the mighty hand of God, that he may exalt you in due time: casting all your care upon him; for he careth for you"* (1 Peter 5:6, 7).

Humble yourself by placing yourself in God's hands and casting the whole of your care upon Him. Hold your tongue. *Don't pull strings to gain position or vie for power—you might get it.* If you wrangle it on your own, then you will have to produce on your own without any help from the Spirit of God. If He didn't place you in a position of honor, He will not sustain you there. *You will be responsible for your own failures.*

You should exalt the Word to such a degree that in every instance God receives all of the credit for whatever is accomplished in your ministry. Let me give you an example. Suppose someone in your congregation should stand up and testify, "I just want to praise the Lord for that car wreck that put me in the hospital because one night I cried out to Him. If it hadn't been for that car wreck, I would have never gotten right with God."

Don't let that kind of testimony go uncorrected in your church. *In love and kindness teach your people not to give credit to disasters for restoring them to God. God's Word will make you right with God—not sickness or disease. It was not the wreck* that spoke to that person and sustained him and revealed God to him. The wreck did not restore him to his health. *It was God's Word* that wrought all these things. The promises were there before the wreck and during his hospital stay and after his release. *Don't give glory to an automobile wreck, to a sickness or disease, or to any other catastrophe or tragedy.* Give the credit to the Word of God for being strong and upholding even in the midst of

Satan's attacks. In doing so, you are magnifying God.

During your church services, if there is ever any doubt about which direction the service is headed, lead it toward the Word. If you are short on time, cut out *everything* except the Word. *Put the Word first.* If you do this, all these other things will take care of themselves.

Jesus said, *"But seek ye first the kingdom of God, and his righteousness; and all these* [other] *things shall be added unto you"* (Matthew 6:33). In order to put the Word first, you will have to feed on it night and day. You must program your mind with it and get rid of all that other rubbish which has been fed into your consciousness. Satan will see to it that it will not be an easy task. *To overcome him, you need an intensive, total immersion of the Word, night and day—not just a casual reading of the Scriptures for a few minutes.*

A music major in college practices for hours every day. Olympic skaters spend six to eight hours a day training for their routines. *We, as ministers, ought to discipline ourselves in the Word 24 hours a day—especially in the beginning years.*

This may well mean that you will have to carry a tape recorder around with you everywhere you go. *Permeate your mind by listening to tapes of the New Testament and good, solid Bible-based sermons. Do whatever it takes to become totally saturated with the Word.* It may mean that you will have your razor in one hand and your tape recorder in the other, or a tape recorder in one hand and a fork in the other. You may have a tape recorder in the car, in the lunch basket, and on the night-stand. You might even use a tape recorder for an alarm clock! This *is meditating on the Word day and night.*

You may say, "I can't do that all the time." Then you'd better think twice about the ministry. If you are not willing, you would be wise just to find some undemanding bureaucratic position in some denominational hierarchy and sit behind a desk and push a pencil. I am not demeaning that type of work or those who fill those positions. I am stressing the fact that if you have made a definite decision to amount to something in the ministry of Jesus Christ and you are determined to take the Great Commission seriously, *then you must be diligent.* You must be prepared to do battle.

I would speak to you no differently if I were your commanding officer about to send you into combat against the best-trained, elite troops of a savage enemy. If you ever find yourself untrained, untaught and suddenly thrust into battle against Satan's storm troops, you will understand the gravity of the situation. *You are God's front-line assault force.* Don't let yourself be deceived about what you are about to confront.

You have an enemy who is doing his dead level best to destroy you. You will be fired upon. If you should be wounded, don't expect to be graciously nursed back to health by sympathetic supporters behind the lines. *In carnal warfare, the wounded are awarded Purple Hearts and are treated as heroes. In the war against Satan, the wounded are often torn to shreds by their own people*. If you fall as a minister, not only will your "loyal" church members not give you a medal, they will probably dishonorably discharge you from service and send you back to selling shoes.

While I was in the service, I asked my sergeant in basic training, "Why are you being so hard on us? Why do we have to train this hard? I can understand the necessity for tough training, but you are the meanest thing on two feet." He looked me straight in the eye and growled, "I'm going to tell you something, boy. When I come walking down the road someplace in the midst of an invasion and find some man lying in the ditch with his guts blown out, its' not going to be my fault!"

The soldiers who survive the war are the ones who take their training seriously. As a "seasoned veteran," I am sharing with you your guarantee of success as a member of God's handpicked storm troops in these last climactic days.

In this crucial, all-out, no-holds-barred offensive, Satan has dispatched hell's choicest personnel to annihilate you and to assure that you never open your mouth to preach the gospel again. He is merciless. He will do everything in his power to destroy everything you have and everything you touch. That is why when the going gets tough, the pressure builds, and it seems like everybody in the world and all hell put together is arrayed against you, *God demands that you walk by the Word and by nothing else.* You will have to go the Word way when it seems like nothing is working. *God's integrity can take the pressure. Just hold tight to the Word.*

Looking to the Word Helps Control Your Flesh

When Gloria and I first started in the ministry, I became more and more aware of God's demand to spend all of my time in the Word—not part of the time, not the majority of it, *all* of it. We carried a tape recorder loaded with gospel material with us everywhere we went. It played all the time.

At that time, we had two small children and were constantly traveling. We preached on the average 21 days each month, twice a day, seven days a week. I did this for the first five years without taking a vacation.

Gloria and I set up the meetings. I ran the tape recorder and the sound system. She helped with the meeting and took care of the kids. After the service, we both sold tapes. We did it all without any help.

After the last meeting, I would excuse myself, go change clothes and dismantle the equipment. It *can* be done with the Word of God going in and out of your consciousness at all times.

After about two years of this, I became so Word oriented that I automatically judged everything I heard or experienced by comparing it to the Word. The Bible became my standard. I retrained myself until the Bible way became habitual.

Hebrews 5:12-14 describes it this way:

For when for the time ye ought to be teachers, ye have need that one teach you again which be the first principles of the oracles of God; and are become such as have need of milk, and not of strong meat. For every one that useth milk is unskillful in the word of righteousness: for he is a babe. But strong meat belongeth to them that are of full age, even those who by reason of use [habit or practice] have their senses exercised [trained] to discern both good and evil.

By staying in the Word, my senses learned to discern between good and evil. My body and mind became so trained that even my flesh rejected evil.

People have the mistaken idea that we have to fight against carnality until Jesus comes to free us. No, that is not so. We must simply walk in the spirit. *The body has no nature of its own. It will do whatever it is told.* People have said, "The nature of God is in your spirit, but the Adamic nature is in your body." *That nature was not Adamic in origin, it was Satanic.*

In the first place, sin was never Adam's nature. Adam had the nature of God. Adam's *original* nature was perfection. Satan's nature took root in him and caused the problem. Adam invited that nature through high treason, but it wasn't in his body. It was in his spirit. His body was trained to follow his spirit.

Your body will do whatever it is trained to do. If your

reborn human spirit dominates your flesh, all of your actions will be godly ones. This can be proven. Let your body stand up or sit down right now without your command. It cannot. It is trained to follow instructions. God created the body in such a way that it could be trained to follow instructions. Your physical body is trained to such a degree that it will function automatically without conscious direction. A well-programmed machine without a nature of its own, your flesh operates totally at your command and for your benefit. You eat, walk, talk, drive and go through a thousand other daily activities with little or no *conscious* thought. But you had to *learn* to do all of these things at one time or another. You have been trained to do them, and your body responds automatically.

At the Fall, Satan took advantage of the fabulous way that God intended the human system to work. He introduced doubt, fear and every other evil thing imaginable until he had programmed man's carnal mind to sin and death.

Man can sin without even thinking about it. Most people have become so proficient at sinning they don't even need to try; it comes quite "naturally"! Their bodies have been trained to do it.

How then can we ever hope to overcome this situation? The answer is found in Romans 12:1-2:

> Present your bodies a living sacrifice, holy, acceptable unto God, which is your reasonable service. And be not conformed to this world: but be ye transformed by the

renewing of your mind, that ye may prove what is that good, and acceptable, and perfect, will of God.

Present your body as a sacrifice to God. Reprogram yourself to automatically act on the Word; your body will be retrained.

By continuing to put the Word of God into your mind and spirit and body, you will eventually come to the place where the Word controls all three. Then the Spirit becomes the dominant force in your life and everything else conforms to it. You will become separated from the world and will have become Word controlled.

God will exalt you as you exalt the Word. Everything will start "coming your way" because of that Word. And as it comes, give it away. *"Give, and it shall be given unto you..."* (Luke 6:38). In this way, you will not only be blessed, you will become a channel of God's blessings to others. *If you are to be a minister in the truest and fullest sense, you must look to the Word day and night.*

Step Six:
Spend Time Fasting

There are two general types of fasts. One type, *a proclaimed fast,* is one which is declared. For instance, a pastor announces that he is calling his entire congregation to voluntarily refrain from food for a certain length of time. The purpose for the fast varies. Most often it is for a time of special prayer.

Another example of a proclaimed fast is a husband and wife who agree to refrain from marital relations for a specific period of time to give themselves to prayer and fasting. Paul speaks of this in 1 Corinthians 7:5, *"Defraud ye not one the other, except it be with consent for a time, that ye may give yourselves to fasting and prayer; and come together again, that Satan tempt you not for your incontinency."* This is a proclaimed fast, a time of mutual consent where both you and your spouse may fast at the same time.

Second Chronicles 20 records a proclaimed fast and the results it achieved. During the reign of Jehoshaphat as king of Judah, word was brought to the king that a vast army was marching toward Jerusalem to attack Judah.

And Jehoshaphat feared, and set himself to seek the Lord, and proclaimed a fast throughout all Judah. And Judah gathered themselves together, to ask help of the Lord: even out of all the cities of Judah they came to seek the Lord (2 Chronicles 20:3-4).

The people were called together into the temple and a fast was declared. They determined not to eat until they had heard from the Lord. Jehoshaphat prayed, leaning on the promises of protection and deliverance God had made to Abraham and his descendants. In answer to his supplication, the Spirit of God spoke through a Levite and gave them instructions. By following the directions, the victory was theirs. *A proclaimed fast will put you in the position to hear from God to receive guidance for a specific situation.*

The other general type of fast is *personal,* one which is not announced to anyone. Always consider your family. The other members of the household may not want to go on a fast with you. Arrangements need to be made for their meals, especially if you are the one who prepares them. (If you are, God will give you the grace to cook the meals for the others without being bothered by it if it's done in love.)

Here are some guidelines: Jesus said, *"Moreover when* (not if—fasting is not optional) *ye fast, be not, as the hypocrites, of a sad countenance: for they disfigure their faces, that they may appear unto men to fast. Verily I say unto you, They have their reward"* (Matthew 6:16).

Hypocritical piety will defeat the purpose of a fast. *If you publicize your spirituality, you will exchange the reward of God for a reward of men.* Their esteem becomes the only recompense you will receive for the effort.

"But thou, when thou fastest, anoint thine head, and wash thy

face; that thou appear not unto men to fast, but unto thy Father which is in secret: and thy Father, which seeth in secret, shall reward thee openly" (Matthew 6:17-18).

This passage of scripture is part of the Sermon on the Mount. Jesus was not primarily teaching on fasting but rather about hypocrisy and pretension. He spoke of giving alms, praying publicly on street corners and fasting. He gave examples of how men ought to worship God in humility, not make a show of their good deeds.

We are not to make our fasting conspicuous. We should dress, groom and conduct ourselves in a normal fashion so that we do not call attention to what we are doing.

The purpose of fasting is not to influence God into acting in our behalf. Abstaining from food does not impress Him. Its purpose is to shut off the influence of our flesh in order to be in tune with the Spirit.

Be careful not to fast in order to receive visions or apparitions from the Lord. I made that mistake, and God sternly reprimanded me for it! He showed me that Satan would love to step in and manifest himself as an angel of light to deceive me (2 Corinthians 11:14). I made a quality decision not to seek visions. Although, if the Father wants to give them to me, that is fine. But I determined that I would base my faith and receive revelation only through the Word of God.

I know one man who supernaturally received revelation about the authority of the believer several years ago. He wanted more of it. Rather than go to the Word of God, he decided that Jesus would have to appear to him in person.

He set himself to fast until Jesus appeared to him. Not having eaten for more than forty days, he came close to dying. Later on, I heard him relate what Jesus had told him. He could have gotten every bit of it out of the book of Ephesians.

After that experience, every time he got into the least bit of trouble, he went right back to the same maneuver. Over a period of time, he departed more and more from the Word of God and began depending on fasting for a vision. Before long he was receiving things that were not from God. He was in so much error that after a while his ministry lost its credibility.

Fasting helps us to receive from God but does not push God to action. We don't have to do anything to move God to exercise His power for us. He has already paid dearly for that privilege. The problem is not God's unwillingness to help us nor His inability to intervene on our behalf. The problem is our spiritual density—our inability to receive what God has already done for us at Calvary.

The problem is not with God. We are the problem. The Transmitter works fine. It's our "receiver" that is not functioning as it should. *Fasting is a tool we use that puts us in a position to be more spiritually aware and "tuned in" to God, so we can better receive from Him.*

Rewards of Fasting

"But thou, when thou fastest, anoint thine head, and wash thy face; [just do what you normally do] *That thou appear not unto men to fast, but unto thy Father which is in secret: and thy Father, which seeth in secret, shall reward thee openly"* (Matthew 6:17-18). *"Shall reward thee openly"*—that is an outright statement of promise right from the lips of Jesus Christ. When you fast, you have a reward coming.

What would that reward be? It is certainly not a pat on the back for not eating. The reward is whatever motivated you to fast. *Whatever it is, establish it by faith and proclaim it before you ever enter the fast. Expect to receive it. God will see in secret and you will receive openly.*

Perhaps you fast for no other reason than to fellowship with God. That is a sound reason, and you will receive your reward of divine fellowship.

You may fast to understand something from the Word that you know God has been trying to reveal to you, but you haven't been able to grasp. That should be the reward you seek in your fast.

Perhaps you have been praying for unsaved family members. You may feel that there should be more you can do to see them converted. Your fast may be undertaken as a time of special intercession.

In this case, you are not trying to motivate God to save them. He has been trying to do that for years. You are simply making a faith connection with the Father, giving Him the opportunity and the faith to get that job accomplished. Establish that as your reward.

This is also true of a proclaimed fast. *Declare the purpose of the fast and **that** will be the reward.*

The Fast God Has Chosen

Isaiah 58 deals with fasting and observance of the Lord's ordinances and the keeping of His Sabbath. In this chapter the Lord says:

> Is not this the fast that I have chosen? to loose the bands of wickedness, to undo the heavy burdens, and to let the oppressed go free, and that ye break every yoke? Is it [God's chosen fast] not to deal thy bread to the hungry, and that thou bring the poor that are cast out to thy house? (verses 6-7).

Why would God tell us to take the food we would have eaten had we not fasted and give it away? We would do this to get the attention of the poor—to bring the poor to your house. For what purpose? *To witness to them about the Lord Jesus Christ. Satisfy their physical hunger first, then feed them spiritually.* Through the new birth and the power of the gospel, you can teach them how to be delivered from poverty.

"*When thou seest the naked, that thou cover him; and that thou hide not thyself from thine own flesh?"* (verse 7).

God is referring to fasting something more than food. He is talking about fasting clothes. You can do without some clothes as well as without food in order to give to someone who has less than you. Consciously put yourself in the position of giving to others.

Verse eight says: *"Then shall thy light break forth as the morning, and thine health shall spring forth speedily: and thy righteousness shall go before thee...."*

What does righteousness have to do with it? Jesus said, *"But seek ye first the kingdom of God, and his righteousness; and all these things shall be added unto you"* (Matthew 6:33). Anything you give away will begin to come back to you.

Don't give away rummage and junk. *Give your good things away. "For with the same measure that ye mete withal it shall be measured to you again"* (Luke 6:38). *"For whatsoever a man soweth, that shall he also reap"* (Galatians 6:7). What you give will determine what you receive. If you give your junk, you will receive junk!

"And thy righteousness shall go before thee; the glory of the Lord shall be thy rearward" (Isaiah 58:8).

The word *rearward* literally means "rear guard" or "rear protection." *As we obey the fast God has chosen, we can take the offensive and know that God is on the defensive in our behalf.*

"Then shalt thou call, and the Lord shall answer; thou shalt cry, and he shall say, Here I am. If thou take away from the midst of

thee the yoke, the putting forth of the finger, and speaking in vanity" (verse 9).

A requirement for the success of the fast God has chosen is to stop judging and accusing others. That kind of talk is all in vain. Let your words always be with grace.

> And if thou draw out thy soul to the hungry, and satisfy the afflicted soul; then shall thy light rise in obscurity, and thy darkness be as the noon day: and the Lord shall guide thee continually, and satisfy thy soul in drought, and make fat thy bones: and thou shalt be like a watered garden, and like a spring of water, whose waters fail not (verses 10-11).

As you are obedient to these scriptures, you will experience an abundance of God's guidance for your life and ministry. You will be fulfilled. The rivers of living water Jesus spoke of will quench your spiritual thirst, and you will have plenty for others to draw on from you.

> And they that shall be of thee shall build the old waste places: thou shalt raise up the foundations of many generations; and thou shalt be called, The repairer of the breach, The restorer of paths to dwell in. If thou turn away thy foot from the sabbath, from doing thy pleasure on my holy day; and call the sabbath a delight,

the holy of the Lord, honourable; and shalt honour
him, not doing thine own ways, nor finding thine own
pleasure, nor speaking thine own words (verses 12-13).

The Sabbath day was the established day of fasting for
Israel. God has not bound us to a certain day in which we are
commanded to fast, but He has instructed us in the way we
should conduct ourselves when we do. *Put pleasures aside.
Meditate on these verses, and consider what God commanded be
done on His day.* Many have missed its true significance. The
day of the week is not as important as we have thought. God
is much more concerned about *how* His people conduct themselves.

*"Then shalt thou delight thyself in the Lord; and I will cause
thee to ride upon the high places of the earth, and feed thee with the
heritage of Jacob thy father: for the mouth of the Lord hath spoken
it"* (verse 14). This happens to be the promise I stood on to
receive the first airplane we needed for the ministry.

What is the "heritage of Jacob" which we are to receive
through fasting? To answer this question let's refer back to
Deuteronomy 32:9-14:

For the Lords' portion is his people; Jacob is the lot of
his inheritance. He found him in a desert land, and in
the waste howling wilderness; he led him about, he
instructed him, he kept him as the apple of his eye. As

an eagle stirreth up her nest, fluttereth over her young, spreadeth abroad her wings, taketh them, beareth them on her wings: So the Lord alone did lead him, and there was no strange god with him. He made him ride on the high places of the earth, that he might eat the increase of the fields; and he made him to suck honey out of the rock, and oil out of the flinty rock; butter of kine, and milk of sheep, with fat of lambs, and rams of the breed of Bashan, and goats, with the fat of kidneys of wheat; and thou didst drink the pure blood of the grape (verses 9-14).

The heritage of Jacob ensures that we hear the voice of the Good Shepherd and that we are not led astray by the evil one. It guarantees our provision of oil for fuel. *It takes gasoline to preach the gospel!*

We are also promised prosperity and abundance in the middle of depression. Those things have already been provided in Christ. Our fasting merely puts us in a better position to receive them because we are not letting our flesh dominate us. *When we truly put God first in every area of our life, then we license Him to be our provider of all things.*

These verses reveal what Jesus meant when He spoke in Matthew 6 about the reward. If done properly, fasting can be beneficial both physically and circumstantially, as well as spiritually. Reap the full benefits of fasting and see the difference it can make in your personal life, as well as in your ministry.

For quick reference, here is an outline of the proper way to fast:

(1) *Decide the purpose of the fast before you begin.*

(2) *Proclaim the fast before the Lord.* Whether proclaimed or personal, it must be declared before God. Otherwise, you will be tempted to break it. This must be a decision of quality. Say, "Father, with You as my helper, in the Name of Jesus, I have settled this today, and until this time tomorrow, food will not pass my lips." Once you have made that *firm* commitment, you will stick by it.

(3) *Believe before the fast that you receive the reward promised by Jesus in Matthew 6:18.* Actually, this assurance is based on Mark 11:24: *"What things soever ye desire, when ye pray, believe that ye receive them, and ye shall have them."* You are not going to receive *because* you fast. You will receive because you *believed* in faith. *Fasting is an assistance to receiving.*

(4) *Minister to the Lord while you are fasting.* Ministering to the Lord in praise and worship will keep your spirit active and build you up. You will need the additional strength to bear up (Colossians 3:16; Ephesians 6:19; Acts 13:1-3).

(5) *Minister to others during and after the fast.* During your fast minister to others only as God leads you to

do so. Always be available. *But remember, fasting is a period of preparing yourself for greater ministry* later on. Afterwards do not think, "Well, I'm never going to fast again. I didn't receive a thing from God during the whole time I was on that fast." Yes, you did. Now, minister to other people, and you will find out that you *have* received. You will witness that the power of God is great upon you!

(6) *Expect assistance from the angels.* Jesus had forty days when He was confronted by Satan on the mount of temptation. After He had successfully resisted Satan's temptation, the Bible tells us, *"Then the devil leaveth him, and, behold, angels came and ministered unto him"* (Matthew 4:11). The angels ministered to Jesus, and you can expect help from ministering servants, too, by faith. Don't *feel* for it. The worst thing you can do is go by your feelings. All they will tell you is, "I'm hungry!" *Shut off your feelings.* Act on your faith. Confess that the angels are attending you. Continue to thank God for it. *They are licensed not only to assist you where you are but also to work for you throughout the world, wherever your influence is needed.*

When you do these things according to God's Word, you will see and reap the results of it for years to come. You will think that you must surely be the most blessed person in the world. Things will come to you for which you have not even prayed or asked God. It has happened to me, and God told me later that these things came to me because I had exalted Him months before. He was working in my behalf, and I was then reaping the fruit of the seed which I had sown. *"Moreover when ye fast...thy Father which is in secret...shall reward thee openly"* (Matthew 6:16-18).

Conclusion:
Formula for Success

I have outlined six steps to excellence in ministry as revealed to me from God's Word. I believe that they will be a blessing to you as you minister the gospel of Jesus Christ. I have personally proven their value and validity over the years in my own ministry.

I would like to share with you a three-step formula for success in applying these principles to your life and ministry. This was given to me years ago by a great man of God. I have tested and proven them many times over. If you will take these truths and apply them seriously, you will have success in every area of your life. Nothing can hold it back from you. *Every Christian endeavor, no matter what it is, will succeed when it is backed with this kind of prayer and dedication because God Himself is behind it.*

(1) *Find the will of God in your situation by prayer and meditation in the Word.* You have a right to know God's plan for your life. *God's Word is His will.* While you are seeking God's will, ask questions of others if you must. Whatever may be involved, find God's plan for your life.

(2) *Once you have determined what the will of God is, confer no more with flesh and blood.* Don't ask any more questions. Don't seek any more advice. Don't hesitate.

Just look to the Word and stand firm on it.

(3) *Get your job done at all costs.* If God has called you to do it, then with God you *can* do it. You are capable of doing *anything* the Word says you can. You are what the Word says you are. Therefore, you can get the job done no matter what the cost. You may find yourself many times in a position in which it will look so much easier to follow anything else other than the Word. Don't do it! *Put God's Word first place in your life and allow it to be final authority. The Word* promises your success. All of heaven's resources—Almighty God, Jesus of Nazareth, the Holy Spirit, all the hosts of heaven—and everything in the Bible promises you THAT YOU WILL GET YOUR JOB DONE! AND GOD WILL BE GLORIFIED IN YOU!

"Now the God of peace, that brought again from the dead our Lord Jesus, that great shepherd of the sheep, through the blood of the everlasting covenant, make you perfect in every good work to do his will, working in you that which is well-pleasing in his sight, through Jesus Christ; to whom be glory for ever and ever. Amen" (Hebrew 13:20-21).

Prayer for Salvation and Baptism in the Holy Spirit

Heavenly Father, I come to You in the Name of Jesus. Your Word says, "Whosoever shall call on the name of the Lord shall be saved" (Acts 2:21). I am calling on You. I pray and ask Jesus to come into my heart and be Lord over my life according to Romans 10:9-10: "If thou shalt confess with thy mouth the Lord Jesus, and shalt believe in thine heart that God hath raised him from the dead, thou shalt be saved. For with the heart man believeth unto righteousness; and with the mouth confession is made unto salvation." I do that now. I confess that Jesus is Lord, and I believe in my heart that God raised Him from the dead.

I am now reborn! I am a Christian—a child of Almighty God! I am saved! You also said in Your Word, "If ye then, being evil, know how to give good gifts unto your children: HOW MUCH MORE shall your heavenly Father give the Holy Spirit to them that ask him?" (Luke 11:13). I'm also asking You to fill me with the Holy Spirit. Holy Spirit, rise up within me as I praise God. I fully expect to speak with other tongues as You give me the utterance (Acts 2:4). In Jesus' Name. Amen!

Begin to praise God for filling you with the Holy Spirit. Speak those words and syllables you receive—not in your own language, but the language given to you by the Holy Spirit. You have to use your own voice. God will not force you to speak. Don't be concerned with how it sounds. It is a heavenly language!

Continue with the blessing God has given you and pray in the spirit every day.

You are a born-again, Spirit-filled believer. You'll never be the same!

Find a good church that boldly preaches God's Word and obeys it. Become part of a church family who will love and care for you as you love and care for them.

We need to be connected to each other. It increases our strength in God. It's God's plan for us.

Make it a habit to watch the *Believer's Voice of Victory* television broadcast and become a doer of the Word, who is blessed in his doing (James 1:22-25).

About the Author

Kenneth Copeland is co-founder and president of Kenneth Copeland Ministries in Fort Worth, Texas, and best-selling author of books that include *How to Discipline Your Flesh* and *Honor—Walking in Honesty, Truth and Integrity*.

Since 1967, Kenneth has been a minister of the gospel of Christ and teacher of God's Word. He is also the artist on award-winning albums such as his Grammy-nominated *Only the Redeemed, In His Presence, He Is Jehovah, Just a Closer Walk* and his most recently released *Big Band Gospel* album. He also co-stars as the character Wichita Slim in the children's adventure videos *The Gunslinger, Covenant Rider* and the movie *The Treasure of Eagle Mountain,* and as Daniel Lyon in the Commander Kellie and the Superkids™ videos *Armor of Light* and *Judgment: The Trial of Commander Kellie.* Kenneth also co-stars as a Hispanic godfather in the 2009 movie *The Rally.*

With the help of offices and staff in the United States, Canada, England, Australia, South Africa, Ukraine and Singapore, Kenneth is fulfilling his vision to boldly preach the uncompromised Word of God from the top of this world, to the bottom, and all the way around. His ministry reaches millions of people worldwide through daily and Sunday TV broadcasts, magazines, teaching audios and videos, conventions and campaigns, and the World Wide Web.

Learn more about Kenneth Copeland Ministries by visiting our website at **kcm.org**

When The LORD first spoke to Kenneth and Gloria Copeland about starting the *Believer's Voice of Victory* magazine...

He said: *This is your seed. Give it to everyone who ever responds to your ministry, and don't ever allow anyone to pay for a subscription!*

For more than 40 years, it has been the joy of Kenneth Copeland Ministries to bring the good news to believers. Readers enjoy teaching from ministers who write from lives of living contact with God, and testimonies from believers experiencing victory through God's Word in their everyday lives.

Today, the *BVOV* magazine is mailed monthly, bringing encouragement and blessing to believers around the world. Many even use it as a ministry tool, passing it on to others who desire to know Jesus and grow in their faith!

Request your FREE subscription to the *Believer's Voice of Victory* magazine today!

Go to **freevictory.com** to subscribe online, or call us at **1-800-600-7395** (U.S. only) or **+1-817-852-6000**.

We're Here for You!®

Your growth in God's WORD and victory in Jesus are at the very center of our hearts. In every way God has equipped us, we will help you deal with the issues facing you, so you can be the **victorious overcomer** He has planned for you to be.

The mission of Kenneth Copeland Ministries is about all of us growing and going together. Our prayer is that you will take full advantage of all The LORD has given us to share with you.

Wherever you are in the world, you can watch the *Believer's Voice of Victory* broadcast on television (check your local listings), the Internet at kcm.org or on our digital Roku channel.

Our website, **kcm.org,** gives you access to every resource we've developed for your victory. And, you can find contact information for our international offices in Africa, Asia, Australia, Canada, Europe, Ukraine and our headquarters in the United States.

Each office is staffed with devoted men and women, ready to serve and pray with you. You can contact the worldwide office nearest you for assistance, and you can call us for prayer at our U.S. number, +1-817-852-6000, 24 hours every day!

We encourage you to connect with us often and let us be part of your everyday walk of faith!

Jesus Is LORD!

Kenneth & Gloria Copeland

Kenneth and Gloria Copeland

CPSIA information can be obtained at www.ICGtesting.com
Printed in the USA
LVOW13s1151110214

373203LV00003B/3/P